Bygone PARTICK

by

BILL SPALDING

The name 'Perdeyc' was first recorded in 1136. Over the centuries at least 17 different ways of spelling the name can be found, the most commonly used being Perthec and later Partic. The meaning of the name has not been established satisfactorily.

First Published in the United Kingdom, 1992
By Richard Stenlake, 1 Overdale Street, Langside, Glasgow G42 9PZ
Tel: 041 632 2304

ISBN 1-872074-20-0

Old Partick

This was one of the last rows of houses in the village to be demolished. It stood at the corner of Dumbarton Road and Keith Street (as this street was re-named in the 1920s). When Partick was a burgh, it had been called Kelvin Street. Before this it was known as 'The Goat' and was more or less the centre of the village. This picture shows 'The Head of the Goat', the Castlebank Street end being known as 'The Foot of the Goat'.

INTRODUCTION

It is appropriate that this book and its companion volume should appear now, as the year 1992 is a double anniversary in the life of Partick.

The history of Partick falls into three distinct periods:
1. PARTICK VILLAGE: from earliest times until 1852.
2. PARTICK BURGH: from 1852 until 1912.
3. PARTICK DISTRICT of the city of Glasgow: from 1912 until today.

There is reason to believe that there was a crossing, probably a ford, over the River Kelvin close to the River Clyde, as far back as Roman times. There is also mention of 'the royal town which is called Pertnich' existing in the 6th century A.D., when King Rhydderch ruled the Kingdom of Strathclyde. The first written reference found so far dates from the dedication of Glasgow Cathedral in 1136. King David granted the lands at 'Perdeyc', a large area on the north of the Clyde, which included present-day Partick, to the Bishops of the Cathedral. They installed the town's mill on the Kelvin, near where Benalder Street road bridge stands today.

By 1834 the population of the village was 1,842, most of whom were weavers. The village was small, being bounded on the south by the Clyde, on the east by the Kelvin and on the north by Dumbarton Road. The western extremity of the village was around about Merkland Street.

The establishment of shipbuilding at the mouth of the Kelvin resulted in a great influx of people mainly from the West Highlands and Ireland. By 1852 the population had grown to over 5,000 and to accommodate these people, the village, now a small industrial town, expanded by building houses north of Dumbarton Road and west of Merkland Street. To make administration easier Partick was declared a burgh in 1852. Its boundaries were drawn up to include: the village, all of Partick West, Whiteinch, Broomhill and Partickhill and the lower part of Dowanhill. Parts of these boundaries are illustrated on pages 3 to 19.

Due to shortage of building space, around 1870, Glasgow began to annexe the surrounding villages and burghs. Being prosperous burghs, Partick and Govan were able to defeat many of the bills which were presented by Glasgow to parliament. But in 1912, they had to admit defeat and they became districts of the City of Glasgow. By this time the population of Partick had risen to around 66,000.

This was at the western boundary of Partick (also of Whiteinch, Glasgow and Lanarkshire). Dumbarton Road became Yoker Road when it crossed the boundary into Scotstoun, which was in Renfrewshire. The boundary was formed by the Whiteinch Burn which ran (and still runs underneath the streets) southwards from Jordanhill, down the west side of Victoria Park Bowling Club, across Dumbarton Road and the eastern part of Connell's shipyard and into the River Clyde. Yoker Road was re-named Dumbarton Road in 1913.

The north bank of the River Clyde, from the mouth of the Whiteinch Burn to the mouth of the River Kelvin, formed the southern boundary of the burgh. This view is a little to the east of the burn and features Barclay Curle's Clydeholm Shipyard which, when it was opened in 1885, was responsible for a rapid increase in the population of Whiteinch. At one time there were several islands, or inches, in the Clyde between Partick Bridge and the Whiteinch Burn. These were later joined to the banks when the river was deepened. The yard was built on the island which had been called Whyt or Whyte Inch. Halfway up and to the right of the picture, the vehicular ferry waits at Linthouse to cross to Whiteinch.

River Clyde at Partick.

The very large building is Meadowside Granary. Built in 1912, it had 13 bays and 13 storeys. In 1936 and 1937 it was extended eastwards and westwards to form a colossal construction with 34 bays. It has not been in use since 1988. Alongside was the Foreign Animal's Wharf and Lairage and Merklands Quay where Partick Thistle once played football. The lairage and the quay had both fallen into disuse by the 1980s.

Mouth of the Kelvin & Govan Ferry.

The eastern boundary ran along the centre of the River Kelvin from its mouth to the Prince of Wales Bridge. To the left of the Govan ferry is the Meadowside Shipyard of D. and W. Henderson. It was built on the old Water Inch and had previously been owned by Tod and McGregor. David Tod was the first Provost of the Burgh. The chain-driven ferry is seen approaching the inclined slipway at the Pointhouse. Circular in shape, it held three carts with horses on a single carriageway in the centre, with 200 passengers at the sides.

KELVIN HALL AND KELVIN BRIDGE, GLASGOW.   204.262.J.V.

The boundary ran across the centre of the Partick road bridge. The Glasgow and Partick coats-of-arms, at their respective ends of the bridge, can still be seen today. Note that this bridge was once known as Kelvin Bridge. The bridge familiar to us today as Kelvin Bridge was at that time known as Great Western Road Bridge.

Rustic Bridge and Kiosk, Kelvingrove Park

Glasgow

The boundary passed behind the Art Galleries where the Clayslaps Mill had stood from at least 1554. It was demolished in the 1870s when the West End Park was being laid out. This view, from the 1901 exhibition, shows the Cabin Tea Rooms on the far side of the river and the bridge leading to the newly-opened Art Galleries. On the hill are the buildings of the Park Circus area.

Kelvingrove Park, Glasgow.

The boundary then ran on beneath this red sandstone bridge on Kelvin Way. It was opened in 1915 to convey traffic from Sauchiehall Street to University Avenue. In 1926 large bronze sculptures, raised on pedestals, were erected at the four corners.

Glasgow. Art Galleries Looking West.

The Kelvin Way Bridge replaced this wrought-iron lattice-girder bridge, which was called the Kelvingrove bridge. It was opened in 1881 to give access to the park and was expanded for the exhibitions of 1901 and 1911.

Kelvingrove Park and University, Glasgow.

225

During the Blitz of March 1941, the balustrade of the Kelvin Way Bridge was shattered and the statues at its northern end were damaged.

Prince of Wales Bridge, Kelvingrove Park   Glasgow

The eastern boundary passed through the park to end at the Prince of Wales Bridge. This splendid forty-foot wide bridge could take two lanes of traffic between its balustrades of Peterhead granite surmounted by lamps. Its predecessor was a wooden bridge of four arches painted to look like masonry. It had been erected temporarily in 1868 for the visit of the Prince of Wales to the University and the site had been chosen to afford him the best view. It was removed when this bridge was opened in June 1895.

Old College Gateway.

The northern boundary started here, at the Old College Gateway and ran westwards across Gilmorehill to reach the junction of University Avenue and Ashton Lane. This meant that there was a portion of the avenue in Partick and it started numbering from Byres Road. The remaining portion was designated University Avenue, Hillhead. It started numbering from the Glasgow end. Thus there were two houses with the address 5 University Avenue etc. Numbering was made continuous from the Glasgow end in 1913. The avenue had previously been part of Dobbie's Loan.

Byres Road, Kelvinside, Glasgow.

K2219 RELIABLE SERIES

Here the northern boundary emerged just above the site of the Grosvenor Cinema and crossed Byres road to run along Albion (Dowanside) Lane. It then zigzagged across Dowanhill enclosing the lower part within the burgh. The name of the road junction, Victoria Cross, can just be seen above the clock in the window on the corner of Dowanside Road; part of Byres Road was once called Victoria Street.

Stonelaw Woods, Public Park, Rutherglen

42782. JV

Wrongly captioned, this postcard shows part of the complex built around the Convent of Notre Dame in Dowanhill. The boundary cut across this site to reach Hyndland Road at the corner of Crown Circus Road North. On the left is the chapel, below which is the school and in the centre is the convent. The teacher training college is just out of the picture to the right. The Observatory stood just behind the site of these buildings until around 1907 when the site was offered for sale.

At Hyndland Road the northern boundary travelled southwards 'along the boundary between the lands of Partickhill and the lands of Hyndland'. This is more or less in line with the present Clarence Lane which runs between Minard Road (now Turnberry Road) and Clarence Drive. Minard Road, seen here, was named in honour of the wife of the local M.P., J. Parker Smith. She was Mary Louisa, daughter of William Hamilton of Minard.

This upper part of Clarence Drive, once called Lancaster Gate, was not in the burgh; the lower part (from the railway bridge to Broomhill Cross) came within the northern boundary. The tram, a yellow number 24, is bound for Langside via Hyndland. The simple Belisha beacon has been replaced with a system of traffic lights.

Dudley Drive, Partick Hill.

Before reaching the bridge in Clarence Drive, the boundary line cut across the eastern end of Dudley Drive to include a small part of it in the burgh. Part of the building on the right was badly damaged by a land-mine during the Blitz of March 1941. 36 people were killed and 21 injured. The restoration of the four closes involved has been so well done that they blend very well with the older part of the building.

CROW ROAD AND STATION BUILDINGS, JORDANHILL

From the bridge in Clarence Drive, the boundary ran northwards to the south-east corner of the grounds of Gartna-vel, before turning west to run along the southern limits of the asylum's grounds. It emerged between the two railway bridges at Jordanhill Station. From there it ran westwards to meet the Whiteinch Burn at Westland Drive and thus complete the circuit of the burgh. The first shop on the right was a branch of the bakery shops of Walter Hubbard, a prominent Partick businessman. Two shops further north is Jordanhill Post Office. Standing outside on the pavement is a small boy who looks like a postboy in his uniform and pill-box hat.

The Cross, Partick.

In the time of the village there were only about six mansion houses on the north side of Dumbarton Road, between Byres road and Balshagray Avenue. The increase in population, caused by the development of the burgh, resulted in the erection of these tenement buildings towards the end of the 1880s. The shops on the left were also replaced by tenements. This part of Dumbarton Road did not exist until the second bridge over the Kelvin was opened in 1797.

Lights with large globes similar to those outside Hepworth's, mark the position of Partick Cross Subway (re-named Kelvinhall). In my younger days the shop with the Hepworth blind was a branch of Bayne and Ducket, a shoe firm which was founded in 1858. George Ducket, son of one of the founders, was educated at the old Partick Academy. Under him, the firm became one of the largest shoe warehousing and distribution networks in Scotland. The clock on the left is still in working order but the little drinking well at the lower left corner (Cooperswell Street) has now vanished.

ST. PETERS BRIDGE ST. GLASGOW

This, the first R.C. Church in Partick, was formally opened in 1858. Bridge Street, at that time, was a toll road leading from Partick Bridge to Partick Cross. The church was closed in 1903 when St. Peter's was opened in Hyndland Street but was re-opened in 1923 due to the rise in population. In 1945 it became a separate parish, St. Simon's. On the right is part of the school which was opened in 1864. It closed in 1924 and the pupils were transferred to Stewartville Street School. The old school building has since been demolished.

When the new church was opened in Hyndland Street, the church in Bridge Street was converted to a billiard room and reading room for the men of the parish. The partitions used to close off the sanctuary can be seen in this photograph of the interior. One of the oldest buildings in Partick, the church and chapel house are still in use. The church is also used by the Polish community of Glasgow.

R. C. Church, Partick

Valentines Series

This picture shows St. Peter's Church, Hyndland Street, the Bridge Street church's larger replacement. The red sandstone building was designed by Pugin and Pugin and holds 1,200 people. The chapel house is on the south-west corner of the site where the children are posing. To the right of this was built a school for girls and infants.

St Peter's Church, Partick.
ARCHBISHOP MAGUIRE preaching at the Jubilee Service
on Sunday, May 23rd, 1908.

The first parish priest (in Bridge Street) had been Father Daniel Gallaugher. When he died, in 1883, he was succeeded by Father John Maguire, who later became Archbishop of Glasgow. Here he is in the pulpit during the Jubilee Service of 1908. Copies of this postcard were sold to raise money for the Memorial Organ Fund.

When St. Peter's in Bridge Street was proving too small to cope with the congregation, some parishioners attended mass at the seminary in Partickhill Road until the church in Hyndland Street was opened. In 1902 the seminary moved to Bearsden. In 1906 St. Kentigern's Hostel (for students) was established in the old seminary building and it was placed under the care of the Marist Brothers.

Byres Road, Glasgow

At one time called 'the South Highway leading from Partick through the village of Byres of Partick', this was the turnpike road leading north from Partick Cross to Great Western Road. For a time the lower part was called Victoria Street and in the 1890s the spellings Byres and Byars were both used. I do not know what the curious structure with the gas lamp on top is, but in later years there was a police call box in this position and this may have been an earlier version. A corner of the splendid Partick Cross Mansions can be seen on the site where the first church building was erected in Partick in 1824 by the Secession Church.

By the 1860s Partick was growing rapidly and with the development of Dowanhill and Partickhill, it was decided to build a new larger church at the junction of Hyndland Street and Hyndland Road. Dowanhill Church was opened in 1899 and has a 195 ft. steeple. In 1983 extensive dry rot was found. A year later the church was bought for a nominal £1 by the Four Acres Charitable Trust with the aim of restoring it for use as a community arts and resource centre. It is now being developed as the Cottier Theatre Project, named after Daniel Cottier who hand-painted the interior of the church.

When Dowanhill Church was opened, a congregation stayed on in the building at Partick Cross as Partick East Church. This new building was erected at the corner of Lawrence Street with Elie Street in 1899. Because of reducing membership and the dry rot, the Dowanhill Church and Partick East congregations united in this building in 1986. A few years later the Old Partick Parish (Established) Church in Church Street closed and its congregation united with Partick East church as Partick Trinity Parish Church.

Dumbarton Road, Partick.

This view looks west from the corner of Dowanhill Street. The left-hand side of the street has hardly changed except that Newton Place Church, with its tall spire, has now gone. On the right, the tenement between Mansfield Street and Hyndland Street has been demolished. Also missing is the lamp further along the pavement from the pillar box. I think this denoted the presence of the chemist's shop (with the mortar and pestle symbol above it). The section of Dumbarton Road on the right, between Mansfield Street and Dowanhill Street, was called Dowanhill Place at one time.

This photograph is taken from the foot of Stewartville Street, looking eastwards along Dumbarton Road. The University tower can be seen in the distance. The District Public Library was built on the right where the gateposts with the large lamp are.

Dumbarton Road, Partick.

RELIABLE WH&S SERIES.

The same stretch of road, this time looking west. This picture is taken from just outside Newton Place (Partick South) Church.

MERKLAND ST PARTICK.

In the time of the village, this was the way to Merklands Farm, which stood just beyond the foot of the street on the site of George Hutcheson's Partick Castle. This was also the way to Steps Road which led to stepping stones over the Kelvin. Much later, in the adjacent Orchard (Vine) Street, the Partick Picture House was built. The subway station was further down on the left. The appearance of Merkland Street today is dominated by the joint entrance to the underground and railway stations.

Dumbarton Road from Peel St. Partick, Looking East.

This photograph shows that traffic congestion is not a modern phenomenon!

Peel Street, named after Sir Robert Peel, was sometimes referred to as 'Rab's Road'. Between the wars, soap-box orators used to stand on its western corner and argue the problems of the day with the passers-by. Free St. Mary's Church is on the right, with Partick High Church beyond the cricket pavilion. The notice board announces a match between the West of Scotland and Drumpellier. The gardens, half-way up on the left, are in front of a terrace which was damaged by the same string of land mines that did so much harm in Dudley Drive.

Hamilton Crescent Cricket Ground, Partick.

The Partick cricket teams of Clutha and Royal used to share this ground. West of Scotland Cricket Club was formed by some of the Clutha players in 1862. From the 1870s until 1939 the ground was also home to the West of Scotland Rugby Club. Perhaps its main claim to fame is that it hosted the first soccer international in 1872. The result was Scotland nil England nil. Houses have now been built within the southern perimeter.

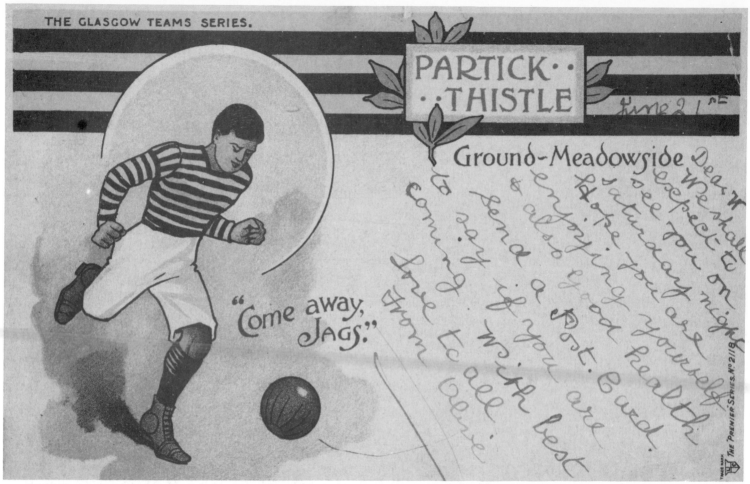

PARTICK··
··THISTLE

Ground-Meadowside

"Come away, JAGS."

The club was formed following the demise of Partick F.C., the original senior club of the district. Their early home games were played on the future site of the Art Galleries, then at Jordanvale Park, then at Muir Park and then at Inchview Park. A new park, situated at Meadowside near where the granary now stands, was opened on 1 September 1897. At that time the team colours were black and yellow hoops. They made their final move to Firhill in 1909. Their main honours (so far) are, winning the Scottish Cup in 1921 (Partick Thistle 1 - Rangers 0) and winning the League Cup in 1971 (Partick Thistle 4 - Celtic 1).

THORNWOOD AVENUE, PARTICK WEST

Most of the earlier buildings in the Thornwood area were built on the grounds of the old Thornwood Mansion.

Horse Ferry Boat, Govan & Partick.

The first ferries from Partick to Govan, in use from 1809, were rowing ferries. In 1867 the hand-operated wagon ferry was replaced by this steam powered craft, which moved from one inclined slipway to the other by pulling itself along a heavy chain laid on the river bed. It travelled from Water Row in Govan to the Pointhouse in Partick from 1867 until 1907 when it was replaced by a steamer which was designed to dock into stairs instead of a slipway. The Partick-Govan ferry ceased to operated in 1966.

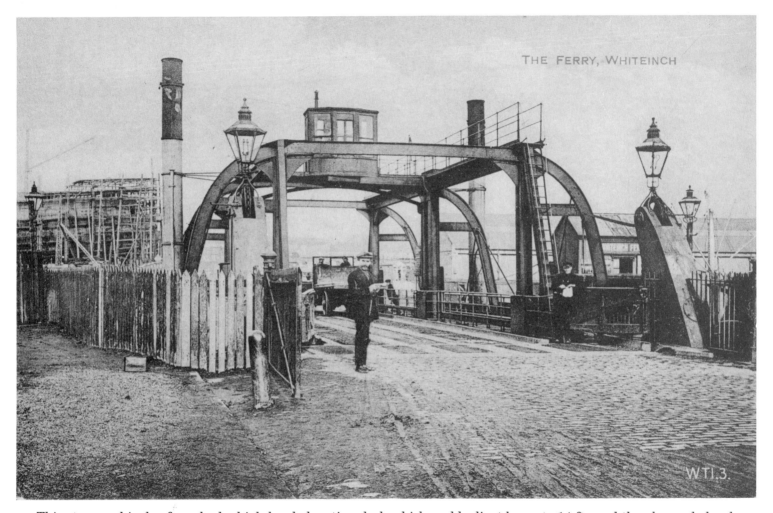

WTI.3.

This steam vehicular ferry had a high-level elevating-deck which could adjust by up to 14 ft., and thus be made level with the quay at any state of the tide. The steam ferry was installed after the recesses in the Clyde had been constructed, replacing an earlier rowing ferry. This crossing was from Barclay Curle's shipyard in Whiteinch to Stephen's shipyard in Linthouse.

The steamer 'Caledonia' sits at Partick Pier at the Pointhouse, beside the slipway for the chain-driven ferry. Prior to 1861 there was no pier at this point and the ferry would lie alongside the steamer to disembark passengers. In April 1861, the steamer 'Lochgoil' arrived off Partick. She was carrying a number of shipyard workers from Napier's who had boarded at Greenock. The ferry, crossing to Partick with four passengers, pulled alongside (against regulations). A large number of the workmen made a reckless surge to board the (rowing) ferry. The crew tried in vain to prevent this, but soon there were 30-40 people aboard the ferry which was meant to carry 24. The ferry overturned, throwing everyone overboard and six people drowned. Shortly after this tragedy the pier was erected.

The Clyde Navigation Trust operated an 'up and down' service within the limits of Glasgow Harbour using the Clutha series of steamers. There were twelve in all and they zigzagged their way, up and down the Clyde, from Stockwell Bridge to Whiteinch, with eight intermediate stops (including Meadowside and Sawmill Road). Because of the fare, they were known as the 'Penny Steamers'. The sailings began in 1884 and ended in November 1903. Their demise was due to the fact that Glasgow Corporation had replaced the horse-drawn trams with electric ones, which passengers found more convenient. This picture shows two Cluthas steaming in opposite directions.

Race for the Cup, Whiteinch Park.

The racing of model boats was very popular in Whiteinch Park. The Victoria Model Yacht Club shared the pond with the New Model Yacht Club.

After the Education Act of 1872, schools in Partick were erected by the Govan Parish School Board. This school was opened in 1896. At the time it was the most costly of these schools and held 1,579 pupils. The site was acquired from the Dowanhill Estate Company. The garden railings were removed during World War II for 'the war effort'.

This building was erected in 1904 for 1,308 pupils and had a swimming pool especially designed for young people and those learning to swim. Children from neighbouring schools also had the use of the pool. It is still used today although Strathclyde Regional Council's Social Work Department occupies the school building. The building replaced Partick Academy, put up in 1850, which provided a high class education to meet the wants of the wealthier class in the community. In 1878 the building was sold to Govan School Board who ran it as Church Street School. The Academy moved to a new building which they built at the top of Peel Street.

Glasgow University Lodge   Partick

This familiar Partick sight shows the entrance to the West End Park on the right, the entrance to the University in the centre and the Western Infirmary entrance on the left. It is little changed today except for the Infirmary entrance. In the days of the village, this site was occupied by a tavern called Burns's Cottage.

This view shows the Sunlight Cottages among the trees. These were built for the 1901 exhibition and are replicas of those at Port Sunlight. Afterwards they were presented to the city by Lord Leverhume and are used as accommodation for park staff. Their addresses are 2 and 4 Dumbarton Road. An Act of Parliament authorised the creation of two new parks in Glasgow because of the expansion of the city. In the preliminary stages the projects were referred to as the West End park and the South Side park (which became Queen's Park). Although the name Kelvingrove Park was officially decided in 1852, the temporary name, West End Park, has never gone out of use.

Many of the streets in this area were given their names by the major landowner, Sir William Hozier, later Lord New-lands of Mauldslie. At first the intention had been to call this street William Street but Hozier decided to name it in honour of Catherine Fielden, who had married Colonel John Hozier in 1824.

Crow Road, Partick.

Apart from sets of traffic lights, Broomhill Cross looks much the same today. In the days of the village this was the turnpike road to Anniesland. For a time the lower part, up to Cross Park, was called Jordanhill Street, but reverted to Crow Road in 1874. The West Highland drovers used to come this way with their animals on their way to the Glasgow markets, stopping at Granny Gibb's Cottage on Dumbarton Road en route. The name Crow Road is thought to come from the Gaelic for cattle or pen.

Marlborough Avenue, Broomhill.

This Street is named after the Churchill family as are some others close by: Blenheim (Churchill) Drive, Randolph Road and Winston (Naseby) Avenue.

Like the tenements round about it, Jordanvale Church was built to cater for the workers of Barclay Curle's. In 1865 Govan Parish Church opened a Whiteinch Church Mission in the sessional school but all church members attended communion in Govan Parish Church. The new church, built in the Scottish Romanesque style, was opened in November 1913.

Whiteinch Homes

These were built around 1890, by the Jane Allan Trust, in the style of English 17th century almshouses. They were used to house elderly employees of the Allan Shipping Line. By 1981 the property had deteriorated and so was sold to the General Trustees of the Church of Scotland, who established the Thomas Chalmers Housing Association to develop and manage the homes. Just beyond it is the Glasgow Institution for Orphan and Destitute Girls.

BALSHAGRAY AVENUE & PARK GARDENS SOUTH BROOMHILL, GLASGOW. 81378.

This magnificent mansion was unfortunately removed to make way for the approach road to the Clyde Tunnel. This is now a very busy area because the side road, (Victoria) Park Gardens South, links the avenue with Crow Road. Behind the house is the spire of Broomhill Trinity Congregational Church. At one time the avenue led from Dumbarton Road to Balshagray House, which stood for nearly 300 years at its northern end.